Merrie Conceited Jests, of George Peele Gentleman, Sometimes Student in Oxford
by George Peele

Copyright © 2019 by HardPress

Address:
HardPress
8345 NW 66TH ST #2561
MIAMI FL 33166-2626
USA
Email: info@hardpress.net

14416
42
(1800)

14416.42

HARVARD COLLEGE
LIBRARY

FROM THE FUND OF
CHARLES MINOT
CLASS OF 1828

MERRIE CONCEITED IESTS,

OF GEORGE PEELE GENTLEMAN, SOMETIMES STVDENT IN OXFORD.

Wherein is shewed the course of his life, how he liued: a man very well knowne in the City of LONDON, and elsewhere.

Buy, reade, and iudge,
The price doe not grudge:
It will doe thee more pleasure,
Than twice so much treasure.

LONDON,
Printed for *Henry Bell*, dwelling in the Little Old Baily in *Eliots* Court.

J. Smeeton, Printer, 148, St. Martin's Lane.

GEORGE PEELE was a Native of Devonshire, from whence being sent to Broadgate's Hall, he was (about the year 1573) made a Student of Christ Church College, Oxford; and in 1579, was admitted to the degree of Master of Arts. After this he removed to London, where he became the City Poet, and had the ordering of the Pageants.

"This person" says Wood "was living in his middle age, in the latter part of Q. Elizabeth's reign, but when or where he died I cannot tell, for so it is and always hath been, that most poets die poor and consequently obscurely, and a hard matter it is to trace them to their Graves." He certainly died in or before the year 1598, as " Meres in the second Part of his Palladis Tamia, or Wits Treasury," printed in that year, mentions the Cause. A List of his Poetical Pieces is given in Ritson's Bibliographia Poetica.

Nash termed him " the chief supporter of pleasance, the Atlas of Poetrie, and *primum verborum artifex*."

The rarity of his " Merrie Conceited Jests" combined with the great price demanded for it, was the chief Inducement to reprint it in its present Form. The Copy made use of for that purpose had belonged to the Rev. J. BRAND, Secretary to the Antiquarian Society; after the Sale of his Library in 1806, it came into the possession of Mr. STACE, and the present Proprietor purchased it in December 1807.

LONDON:
Reprinted for S. W. SINGER, 13, ST. JAMES's STREET;
AND
R. TRIPHOOK, 37, ST. JAMES's STREET.
1809.

The Iests of GEORGE PEELE, with foure of his Companions at *Brainford*.

Eorge, with others of his Associates, being merry together at the Tauerne, hauing more store of Coine than usually they did possesse, although they were as regardelesse of their siluer, as a garden whore is of her honesty, yet they intended for a season to become good husbands, if they knew how to be sparing of that their pockets were then furnisht withall: Five pounds they had amongst them, and a plot must be cast how they might be merry with extraordinary cheare three or foure dayes, and keepe their five pounds whole in stocke: *George Peele* was the man must doe it, or none, and generally they coniurde him by their loues, his owne credit, and the reputation that went on him, that he would but in this shew his wit: and withall he should haue all the furtherance that in them lay. *George* as easie as they earnest to be wonne to such an exploit, consented, and gathered their mony together, and gaue it all to *George*, who should be their Purse-bearer, and the other foure should seeme as seruants to *George Peele*; and the better to colour it, they should goe change their cloaks, the one like the other, so neere as they could possible:

the

the which at *Belzebubs* brother the Brokers, they might quickly doe: This was foone accomplifhed, and *George* was furnifhed with his blacke Sattin fuit, and a paire of boots, which were as familiar to his legs, as the Pillory to a Bakers or Colliers necke, and he fufficiently poffeft his friends with the whole fcope of his intent, as, gentle Reader, the fequell will fhew. Inftantly they tooke a paire of Oares, whofe armes were to make a falfe gallop no further than *Brainford*, where their fare was paid them fo liberally, that each of them the next tide to *London*, purchafed two new waftcoats, yet fhould thefe good benefactors come to their ufuall places of trade, and if they fpie a better fare than their owne, that haply the Gentleman hath more minde to goe withall, they will not onely fall out with him that is of their owne fweet tranfporters, as they are: but abufe the faire with foule fpeeches, as, a Pox, or the Deuill goe with you, as their Godfather *Caron* the Ferry-man of Hell hath taught them. I fpeake not this of all, but of fome that are brought vp in the Eaft, fome in the Weft, fome in the North; but moft part in the South: but for the reft they are honeft compleat men, leauing them to come to my honeft *George*, who is now merry at the three Pigeons in *Brainford*, with Sack and Sugar, not any wine wanting, the Muficians playing, my hoft drinking, my hoftis dancing with the worfhipfull Juftice, for fo then he was termed, and his manfion houfe in *Kent*, who came thither of purpofe to be merry with his men, becaufe he could not fo conueniently neare home, by reafon of a fhrewifh wife he had: my gentle hoftis gaue him all the entertainment her houfe could afford; for Mafter *Peele* had paid royally, for all his fiue pounds was come to ten groats. Now *George Peeles* wit labours to bring in that fiue pounds there was fpent, which was foone begotten. Being fet at dinner, My Hoft, quoth
George,

George, how fals the Tide out for *London*? Not till the euening, quoth mine Hoſt, haue you any buſineſſe ſir? Yes marry, quoth *George*, I intend not to go home this two dayes: Therefore my Hoſt ſaddle my man a horſe for *London*, if you be ſo well furniſhed, for I muſt ſend him for one bag more, quoth *George*, ten pounds hath ſeene no Sunne this ſix mōneths. I am ill furniſhed if I cannot furniſh you with that, quoth my Hoſt, and preſently ſadled him a good Nag, and away rides one of *Georges* men to *London*, attending the good houre of his Maſter *Peele* in *London*. In the meane time *George* beſpeaks great cheare to ſupper, ſaying, he expected ſome of his friends from *London*. Now you muſt imagine there was not a penny owing in the houſe, for he had paid as liberally as Cæſar, as farre as Cæſars wealth went. For indeed moſt of the mony was one Cæſars an honeſt man yet liuing in *London*. But to the Cataſtrophe. All the day before, had one of the other men of *George Peele* beene a great ſoliciter to my Hoſtis, ſhe would beg leaue of his Maſter he might goe ſee a maid, a ſweet heart of his ſo farre as *Kingſtone*, and before his Maſter went to bed he would returne againe: ſaying, he was ſure ſhe might command it at his Maſters hands. My kinde Hoſtis willing to pleaſure the young fellow, knowing in her time what belonged to ſuch matters, went to Maſter *Peele*, and moued him in it, which he angerly refuſed: but ſhe was ſo earneſt in it, that ſhe ſwore he ſhould not deny her, proteſting he went but to ſee an Uncle of his ſome five miles off: Marie I thanke you, quoth *George*, my good Hoſtis, would you ſo diſcredit me, or hath the knaue no more wit, than at this time to goe, knowing I haue no horſe here, and would the baſe cullian goe a foot? Nay, good ſir, quoth mine Hoſtis, be not angry, it is not his intent to goe a foot: for he ſhall haue my Mare, and I will aſſure you Sir,

upon

upon my word he shall be here againe to haue you to bed; well, quoth *George*, Hostis, Ile take you at your word, let him go, his negligence shall light upon you. So be it, quoth mine Hostis: so downe goeth she, and sends away ciuill *Thomas*, for so she cald him, to his sweet heart backt upon her Mare: which *Thomas* in stead of riding to *Kingstone*, tooke *London* in his way, where meeting with my other horseman, attended the arriuall of *George Peele*, which was not long after: they are at *London*, *George* in his chamber at *Brainford*, accompanied with none but one *Anthony Nit* a Barber, who din'd and supt with him continually, of whom he had borrowed a Lute to passe away the melancholy afternoone, of which he could play as well as *Bankes* his horse. The Barber very modestly takes his leaue, *George* obsequiously bids him to supper, who (God willing) would not faile. *George* being left alone with his two supposed men, gaue them the meane how to escape, and walking in the court, *George* found fault with the weather, saying it was rawish and cold: which word mine Hostis hearing, my kinde Hostis fetched her husbands holiday gowne, which *George* thankfully put about him, and withall called for a cup of Sacke, after which he would walke into the Meddowes and practise upon his Lute. 'Tis good for your worship to do so, quoth mine Hostis: which walke *George* tooke directly to *Sion*, where hauing the aduantage of a paire of Oares at hand, made this iourny for *London*, his two Associates behind had the plot in their heads by *Georges* instruction for their escape: for they knew he was gone, my Hostis she was in the market buying of prouision for supper: mine Host he was at Tables, and my two masterlesse men desired the maids to excuse them if their Master came, for, quoth they, we will goe drinke two pots with my Smug Smiths wife at old *Brainford*. I warrant you, quoth the Maids.

So

So away went my men to the Smiths at old *Brainford*, from thence to *London*; where they all met, and fold the Horfe and the Mare, the Gowne and the Lute, which mony was as badly fpent, as it was lewdly got. How my Hoft and my Hoftis lookt when they faw the euent of this; goe but to the three Pigeons at *Brainford*, you fhall know.

The Iefts of *George* and the *Barber*.

GEorge was not fo merry at *London* with his Capons and Claret, as poore *Anthony* the Barber was forrowfull at *Brainford* for the loffe of his Lute, and therefore determined to come to *London* to feeke out *George Peele*, which by the meanes of a kinfman that *Anthony Nit* had in *London*, his name was *Cuts* or *Feats*, a fellow that had good fkill in tricks on the Cards, and he was well acquainted with the place where *Georges* common abode was: and for kindred fake he directed the Barber where he fhould haue him, which was at a blinde Alehoufe in Sea-coale lane. There he found *George* in a greene Jerkin, a Spanifh platter fafhioned hat, all alone at a peck of Oyfters. The Barbers heart danc't within him for ioy he had fo happily found him, he gaue him the time of the day: *George* not a little abafhed at the fight of the Barber, yet went not to difcouer it openly, he that at all times had a quick inuention, was not now behind hand to entertaine my Barber, who knew for what his comming was: *George* thus faluted him, My honeft Barber, quoth *George*, welcome to *London*, I partly know your bufineffe, you come for your Lute, doe you not? Indeed Sir, quoth the Barber, for that is my comming. And belieue me, quoth *George*, you fhall not lofe your labour; I pray you ftand to and eat an Oyfter, and Ile goe with you presently:

presently: For a Gentleman in the City of great worship, borrowed it of me for the vse of his Daughter, that playes exceeding well, and had a great desire to haue the Lute: but, sir, if you will goe along with me to the Gentlemans house, you shall haue your Lute with great satisfaction, for had not you come, I assure you I had sent to you, for you must vnderstand, that all that was done at *Brainford* among us mad Gentlemen, was but a iest, and no otherwise. Sir, I thinke not any otherwise, quoth the Barber: but I would desire your worship, that as you had it of me in loue, so in kindnesse you would helpe me to it againe. Oh God, what else, quoth *George*, Ile goe with thee presently, euen as I am, for I came from Hunting this morning; and should I goe up to the certaine Gentlemen aboue, I should hardly get away. I thank you sir, quoth the Barber, so on goes *George* with him in his green Jerkin, a wand in his hand very pretty, till he came almost at the Aldermans house, where making a sodaine stay, Afore God, quoth *George*, I must craue thy pardon at this instant, for I haue bethought my selfe, should I goe as I am, it would be imagined I had had some of my Lords hounds out this morning, therefore Ile take my leaue of thee, and meet thee where thou wilt about one of the clocke. Nay good sir, quoth the Barber, go with me now: for I purpose, God willing, to be at *Brainford* to night. Saist thou so, quoth *George*, why then Ile tell thee what thou shalt doe: thou art here a stranger, and altogether vnknowne, lend me thy cloake and thy hat, and do thou put on my greene Jerkin, and Ile go with thee directly along. The Barber loth to leaue him untill he had his Lute, yeelded to the change. So when they came to the Gentlemans porch, he put on *Georges* greene Jerkin, and his Spanish hat, and he the Barbers cloake and his hat. Either of them being thus fitted, *George* knocks at the doore, to

whom

whom the Porter bids heartily welcome, for *George* was well knowne, who at that time had all the ouersight of the Pageants; he desires the Porter to bid his friend welcome, for he is a good fellow and a keeper, M. Porter, one that at his pleasure can bestow a haunch of Venison on you; Marry that can I, quoth the Barber. I thanke you sir, answered the Porter, *M. Peele*, my Master is in the Hall, pleaseth it you to walke in? With all my heart, quoth *George*, in the meane time let my friend beare you company. That he shall M. *Peele*, quoth the Porter, and if it please him he shall take a simple dinner with me. The Barber giues him hearty thanks, not misdoubting M. *Peele* any way, seeing him known; and himselfe so welcome; fell in chat with the Porter. *George Peele* goes directly to the Alderman, who now is come into the Court; in the eye of the Barber, where *George* after many complaints, draws a blacke paper out of his bosome, and making action to the Barber reads to the Alderman, as followeth; I humbly desire your worship to stand my friend, in a sleight matter, yonder hard fauoured knaue, that sits by your Worships Porter, hath dog'd me to arrest me, and I had no other means but to take your worships house for shelter, the occasion is but triuiall, only for stealing of a peece of flesh, my selfe consorted with 3. or 4. Gentlemen of good fashion, that would not willingly haue our names come in question. Therefore this is my boone, that your worship would let one of your seruants let mee out at the Garden doore, and I shall thinke my selfe much indebted to your Worship. The kinde Gentleman little dreaming of *George Peeles* deceit, tooke him into the Parlor, gaue him a brace of Angels, and caused one of his seruants to let *George* out at the Garden doore; which was no sooner opened, but *George* made way for the Barber seeing him any more, and all the way he went could not chuse but

B   laugh

laugh at his knauish conceit, how he had guld the simple Barber, who sate all this while with the Porter blowing of his nailes: to whom came this fellow that let out *George*. You whorson Keeperly Rascall, quoth the fellow, doe you come to arrest any honest Gentleman in my Masters house? Not I, so God helpe me, quoth the Barber, I pray sir where is the Gentleman M. *Peele* that came along with me? Farre enough, quoth the fellow, for your comming neere him, he is gone out at the Garden doore. Garden doore, quoth the *Barber*, why, haue you any more doores than one? We haue sir, and get you hence or Ile set you going goodman Keeper. Alas, quoth the *Barber*, sir I am no Keeper, I am quite vndone: I am a *Barber* dwelling at *Brainford*, and with weeping teares vp and told him how *George* had vsed him. The seruant goes in and tels his Master: which when he heard, he could not but laugh at the first: yet in pitty of the poore *Barber*, he gaue him twenty shillings towards his losse. The *Barber* sighing tooke it, and towards *Brainford* home he goes, and whereas he came from thence in a new Cloake and a faire Hat, he went home weeping in an old Hat, and a greene Jerkin.

How *George Peele* became a Physician.

GEorge on a time being happily furnished both of horse and mony, though the horse he hired, and the money he borrowed: but no matter how he was possest of them: and towards *Oxford* he rides to make merrie with his friends and fellow students: and in his way he tooke vp *Wickham*, where he soiourned that night: being at supper, accompanied with his Hostis, among other table-talke, they fell into discourse of Chirurgerie, of which my Hostis was a simple professour. *George Peele* obseruing

the

the humour of my shee Chirurgian; vpheld her in all the strange cures she talked of, and praised her womanly endeuour; telling her, he loued her so much the better, becaufe it was a thing that he profeſſed, both Phyſicke and Chirurgerie: and *George* had a Dictionarie of Phyſicall words, that it might set a better gloſſe vpon that which he feemingly profeſt: and told his good Hoſtis at his returne he would teach her something that ſhould doe her no hurt: for (quoth he) at this inſtant I am going about a great Cure as farre as *Warwick-ſhire*, to a Gentleman of great liuing, and one that hath beene in a Conſumption this halfe yeare, and I hope to doe him good. O God (quoth the Hoſtis) there is a Gentleman not a quarter of a Mile off, that hath beene a long time ſicke of the ſame diſeaſe: Beleeue me, ſir, quoth the Hoſtis, would it pleaſe your worſhip e're your departure in the morning, but to viſit the Gentleman, and but ſpend your opinion of him, and I make no queſtion but the Gentlewoman will be very thankfull to you. I faith (quoth *George*) haply at my returne I may; but at this time my haſte is ſuch that I cannot: and ſo good night mine Hoſtis. So away went *George* to bed; and my giddy Hoſtis, right of the nature of moſt women, thought that night as long as ten, till ſhe was deliuered of that burthen of newes which ſhe had receiued from my new Doctor: (for ſo he termed himſelf.) Morning being come, at breake of the day mine Hoſtis trudges to this Gentlemans houſe, acquainted his wife what an excellent man ſhe had at her houſe: proteſting he was the beſt ſeene in Phyſicke, and had done the moſt ſtrangeſt cures that euer ſhe heard of: ſaying that if ſhe would but ſend for him, no queſtion he would do him good. The gentlewoman glad to heare of any thing that might procure the health of her Huſband, preſently ſent one of her men to deſire the Doctor to come and viſit her

Huſband:

Husband: Which message when *George* heard, he wondred, for he had no more skill in Physicke, than in Musicke, and they were as distant both from him, as heauen from hell. But, to conclude, *George* set a bold face on it, and away went he to the sicke Gentleman; where when he came, after some complement to the Gentlewoman, he was brought to the Chamber, where the ancient Gentleman lay wonderfull sicke, for all Physicke had giuen him ouer: *George* begins to feele his Pulses, and his Temples, saying, he was very farre spent: yet, quoth he, vnder God, I wil doe him some good, if Nature be not quite extinct. Whereupon he demanded whether they had euer a Garden? That I haue, quoth the Gentlewoman. I pray you direct me thither, quoth *George*: Where when he came, he cut a handful of euery flower, herb and blossome, or whatsoeuer else in the Garden, and brought them in the lapid of his cloake, boyled them in Ale, strained them, boiled them againe; and when he had all the iuyce out of them, of which he made some pottle of drinke, he caused the sicke Gentleman to drinke off a maudlin Cupfull, and willed his wife to giue him of that same at morning, noone, and night: protesting, if any thing in this world did him good, it must be that: giuing great charge to the Gentlewoman to keepe him wonderfull warme: and at my returne, quoth *George*, some ten daies hence, I will returne and see how he fares: For, quoth he, by that time some thing will be done, and so I will take my leaue. Not so, quoth the Gentlewoman, your worship must needs stay and take a simple dinner with me to day. Indeed, quoth *George*, I cannot now stay; my haste is such, I must presently to Horse. You may suppose *George* was in haste vntill he was out of the Gentlewomans house: for he knew not whether he had poysoned the Gentleman or not, which made him so eager to be gone out of the Gentlemans house.

house. The Gentlewoman seeing she could by no meanes stay him gaue him two brace of Angels, which neuer shined long in his purse, and desired him at his returne to know her house: which *George* promised, and with seeming nicenesse took the gold, and towards Oxford went he, forty shillings heauier than he was, where he brauely domineered while his Physicall money lasted. But to see the strangenesse of this: Whether it was the vertue of some herbe which he gathered, or the conceit the Gentleman had of *George Peele*, but it so pleased God the Gentleman recouered; and in eight daies walked abroad; and that fortunate potion which *George* made at randome, did him more good than many pounds that he had spent in halfe a yeare before in Physicke. *George* his money being spent, he made his returne towards London; and when he came within a mile of the Gentlemans house, he inquired of a countrey fellow how such a Gentleman did. The fellow told him God be praised, his good Landlord was well recouered by a vertuous Gentleman that came this way by chance. Art thou sure of it, quoth *George*? Yes, beleeue me, quoth the fellow; I saw him in the fields but this morning. This was no simple newes to *George*. He presently set spurres to his Horse, and whereas hee thought to shun the towne, he went directly to his Inne: at whose arriuall, the Hostis clapt her hands, the Oastler laught, the Tapster leapt, the Chamberlaine ran to the Gentlemans house, and told him the Doctor was come. How ioyfull the Gentleman was, let them imagine that haue any after-healths. *George Peele* was sent for, and after a million of thanks from the Gentleman, and his friends, *George Peele* had twenty pounds deliuered him: which money, how long it was a spending, let the Tauernes in *London* witnesse.

How

How *George* helped his friend to a Supper.

GEorge was inuited one night by certaine of his friends to supper, at the White Horse in Friday Street; and in the Euening as he was going, he met with an old friend of his, who was so ill at the stomacke, hearing *George* tel him of the good cheere he went to, himselfe being vnprouided both of meat and mony, that he swore he had rather haue gone a mile about than haue met him at that instant. And beleeue me, quoth *George*, I am hartily sorry that I cannot take thee along with me, my selfe being but an inuited guest; besides, thou art out of cloathes, vnfitting for such a company: Marry this Ile doe, if thou wilt follow my aduice, Ile helpe thee to thy supper. Any way, quoth he to *George*, doe thou but deuise the meanes, and Ile execute it. *George* presently told him what he should doe; so they parted. *George* well entertained, with extraordinary welcome, and seated at the vpper end of the Table, Supper being brought vp, H. M. watched his time below; and when he saw that the meat was carried vp, vp he followes, (as *George* had directed him,) who when *George* saw, You whorson Rascall (quoth *George*) what make you here? Sir, quoth he, I am come from the party you wot of. You Rogue, (quoth *George*) haue I not forewarned you of this? I pray you, Sir, quoth he, heare my Errand. Doe you prate, you slaue, quoth *George*, and with that tooke a Rabbet out of the Dish, and threw it at him. Quoth he, you vse me very hardly. You Dunghill, quoth *George*, doe you out-face me? and with that tooke the other Rabbet, and threw it at his head; after that a Loafe; then drawing his dagger making an offer to throw it, the Gentlemen staid him: meane while H. M. got the Loafe and the two Rabbets, and away he went:

went: which when *George* saw he was gone, after a little fretting, he sate quietly. So by that honest shift he helped his friend to his supper, and was neuer suspected for it of the company.

How *George Peele* was shauen, and of the reuenge he tooke.

THere was a Gentleman that dwelt in the West Countrey, and had stayed here in *London* a Tearme longer than hee intended, by reason of a Booke that *George* had to translate out of Greeke into English: and when he wanted money, *George* had it of the Gentleman: but the more he supplied him of Coine, the further off he was from his Booke, and could get no end of it, neither by faire meanes, entreaty, or double paiment; for *George* was of the Poetical disposition, neuer to write so long as his mony lasted, some quarter of the booke being done, and lying in his hands at randome: The Gentleman had plotted a means to take such an order with *George* next time hee came, that hee would haue his Booke finished. It was not long before he had his company; his arriuall was for more mony: the Gentleman bids him welcome, causeth him to stay dinner, where falling into discourse about his Booke, found that it was as neere ended as he left it two moneths agoe. The Gentleman, meaning to be guld no longer, caused two of his men to binde *George*, hand and foot in a Chaire: a folly it was for him to aske what they meant by it: the Gentleman sent for a Barber, and *George* had a beard of an indifferent size, and well growne, he made the Barber shaue him beard and head, left him as bare of haire, as he was of money: the Barber he was well contented for his paines, who left *George* like an old woman in mans apparell; and his voyce became it well,

well, for it was more woman than man. *George*, quoth the Gentleman, I haue alwaies vfed you like a friend, my purfe hath beene open to you; that you haue of mine to tranflate, you know it is a thing I highly efteeme, therefore I haue vfed you in this fafhion, that I might haue an end of my Booke, which fhall be as much for your profit as my pleafure. So forthwith he commanded his men to vnbinde him, and putting his hand into his pocket, gaue him two brace of Angels: quoth he, M. *Peele*, drinke this, and by that time you haue finifhed my booke, your beard will be growne, vntill which time I know you will be afhamed to walke abroad. *George* patiently tooke the gold, faid little, and when it was darke night, tooke his leaue of the Gentleman, and went directly home: who when his wife faw, I omit the wonder fhe made, but imagine thofe that fhall behold their hufbands in fuch a cafe. To bed went *George*, and ere morning he had plotted fufficiently how to cry *quid pro quo* with his politicke Gentleman.

The Ieft of *George Peele* at *Briftow*.

GEorge was at Briftow, and there ftaying fome what longer than his coine would laft him, his Palfrey that fhould be his Carrier to *London*, his head was growne fo big, that he could not get him out of the ftable. It fo fortuned at that inftant, certaine Players came to the Towne, and lay at that Inne where *George Peele* was: to whom *George* was well knowne, being in that time an excellent Poet, and had acquaintance of moft of the beft Plaiers in *England*; from the triuiall fort he was but fo fo; of which thefe were, onely knew *George* by name, no otherwife. There was not paft three of the company come with the Carriage, the reft were behinde, by reafon of

of a long Journey they had, so that night they could not
enact, which *George* hearing, had presently a Stratageme
in his head to get his Horse free out of the stable, and
Money in his purse to beare his charges vp to *London*.
And thus it was: He goes directly to the Mayor, tels
him he was a Scholler and a Gentleman, and that he had
a certaine History of the Knight of the Rodes; and
withall, how *Bristow* was first founded and by whom,
and a briefe of all those that before him had succeeded in
Office in that worshipfull Citie: desiring the Mayor, that
he with his presence, and the rest of his Brethren, would
grace his labours. The Mayor agreed to it, gaue him
leaue, and withall appointed him a place, but for himselfe
he could not be there, being in the euening: but bade
him make the best benefit he could of the Citie, and
very liberally gaue him an Angel, which *George* thankfully
receiues, and about his businesse he goes, got his stage
made, his History cried, and hired the Players Apparell,
to florish out his Shew, promising to pay them liberally;
and withall desired them they would fauour him so much,
as to gather him his money at the doore, (for hee thought
it his best course to imploy them, lest they should spie
out his knauery, for they haue perillous heads.) They
willingly yeeld to do him any kindnesse that lies in them;
in briefe, carry their apparell to the Hall, place them-
selues at the doore, where *George* in the meane time with
the ten shillings he had of the Mayor, deliuered his horse
out of Purgatory, and carries him to the townes end, and
there placeth him, to be ready at his comming. By this
time the Audience were come, and so forty shillings
gathered, which money *George* put in his purse, and
putting on one of the Players silke Robes, after the Trum-
pet had sounded thrice, out he comes, makes low obey-
sance, goes forward with his Prologue, which was thus:

C   *A tri-*

A trifling Toy, a Iest of no account, pardie.
The Knight, perhaps you thinke for to be I:
Thinke on so still; for why you know that thought is free,
Sit still a while, Ile send the Actors to yee.

Which being said, after some fire workes that he had made of purpose, threw out among them, and downe staires goes he, gets to his Horse, and so with fortie shillings to *London*; leaues the Players to answer it; who when the Jest was knowne, their innocence excused them, being as well gulled as the Maior and the Audience.

How *George* gulled a Punke, otherwise called a Croshabell.

COmming to *London*, hee fell in company with a Cockatrice; which pleased his eye so well, that *George* fell aboording of her, and proffered her the wine: which my Croshabell willingly accepted: to the Tauerne they go, where after a little idle talke, *George* fell to the question about the thing you wot of. My she-Hobby was very dainty, which made *George* farre more eager; and my lecherous animall proffered largely to obtaine his purpose. To conclude, nothing she would grant vnto except ready coine, which was forty shillings, not a farthing lesse: if so he would, next night she would appoint him where he should meet her. *George* saw how the game went, that she was more for lucre than for loue, thus cunningly answered her: Gentlewoman, howsoeuer you speake, I do not thinke your heart agrees with your tongue; the money you demand is but to trie me, and indeed but a trifle to mee: but because it shall not be

said

said I bought that Iemme of you I prize so highlie, Ile giue you a token to morrow, that shall be more worth than your demand, if so you please to accept it. Sir, quoth shee, it contenteth me well: and so, if please you, at this time weele part, and to morrow in the euening meet you where you shall appoint. The place was determined, and they kist and parted, she home, *George* into Saint Thomas Apostles, to a friend of his, of whom he knew he could take vp a peticoat of trust: (the first letter of his name begins with *G*.) A Peticoat he had of him, at the price of fiue shillings; which money is owing till this day. The next night being come, they met at the place appointed, which was a Tauerne: there they were to suppe: that ended, *George* was to goe home with her, to end his Yeomans plee in her common case. But Master *Peele* had another drift in his mazzard: for he did so ply her with wine, that in a small time she spun such a threed, that she reeled homewards, and *George* he was faine to be her supporter: when to her house she came, with nothing so much painting in the inside, as her face had on the outside; with much ado her maide had her to bed, who was no sooner layd, but she fell fast asleepe; which when *George* perceiued, he sent the maide for Milke, and a quart of Sacke to make a Posset; where before her returne, *George* made so bold as to take vp his owne new Petticoat, a faire Gowne of hers, two gold Rings that lay in the window, and away he went: the Gowne and the gold Rings he made a chaffer of; the Petticoat he gaue to his honest wife, one of the best deeds he euer did to her. How the Croshabell lookt when she awaked and saw this, I was neuer there to know.

How the Gentleman was gulled for shauing of *George*.

GEorge had a Daughter of the age of tenne yeers, a Girle of a prettie forme, but of an excellent wit: all part of her was Father, saue her middle: and she had *George* so tutored all night, that although himselfe was the Author of it, yet had he beene transformed into his Daughters shape, he could not haue done it with more conceit. *George* at that time dwelt at the Bank-side, from whence comes this she-sinnow, early in the morning with her haire disheuelled, wringing her hands, and making such pitifull moane with shrikes and teares, and beating of her brest, that made the people in a maze: some stood wondering at the Childe, others plucked her to know the occasion; but none could stay her by any meanes, but on she kept her iourney, crying, O, her Father, her good Father, her deare Father, ouer the Bridge, thorow Cheape-side, and so to the Old Bailey, where the Gentleman soiourned, there sitting her selfe downe, an hundred people gaping vpon her, there she begins to cry out, Woe to that place, that her Father euer saw it, shee was a cast-away, her Mother was vndone, till with the noyse, one of the Gentlemans men comming downe, looked on her, and knew her to bee *George Peeles* Daughter: hee presently runnes vp, and tels his Master: who commanded his man to bring her vp. The Gentleman was in a cold sweat, fearing that *George* had for the wrong he did him the day before, some way vndone himselfe. When the Girle came vp, he demanded the cause why she so lamented, and called vpon her Father? *George* his flesh and bloud, after a million of sighes, cried out vpon him, he had made her Father, her good father, drowne himselfe. Which words

words once vttered, she fell into a counterfeit swoone, whom the Gentleman soone recouered. This newes went to his heart, and he being a man of a very mild condition, cheered vp the Girle, made his men to go buy her new cloathes frō top to toe, said he would be a father to her, gaue her fiue pounds, bid her go home and carry it to her mother, and in the euening he would visit her: At this, by little and little she began to be quiet, desiring him to come and see her Mother. He tels her he will not faile, bids her goe home quietly. So downe staires goes she peartly, and the wondring people that staid at doore to heare the manner of her griefe, had of her nought but knauish answers, and home went she directly. The Gentleman was so crossed in minde, and disturbed in thought at this vnhappy accident, that his soule could not be in quiet till he had beene with this wofull widdow, as he thought, and presently went to *Blacke Friers*, tooke a paire of Oares, and went directly to *George Peeles* house, where he found his Wife plucking of Larks, my crying Crocadile turning of the spit, and *George* pind vp in a blanket at his translation. The Gentleman, more glad at the unlookt for life of *George*, than the losse of his money, tooke part of the good cheere *George* had to supper, wondred at the cunning of the Wench, and within some few daies after had an end of his Booke.

How *George* read a Play-booke to a Gentleman.

THere was a Gentleman, whom God had indued with good liuing to maintaine his small wit: he was not a Foole absolute, although in this world he had good fortune: and he was in a manner an Ingle to *George*, one that tooke great delight to haue the first hearing of any worke that *George* had done, himselfe being a Writer, and

and had a Poeticall inuention of his owne, which when he had with great labour finished, their fatall end was for priuy purposes. This selfe-conceited brocke had *George* inuented to halfe a score sheets of Paper; whose Christainly pen had writ *Finis* to the famous Play of the Turkish *Mahomet,* and *Hyrin* the faire Greeke, in Italian called a Curtezan, in Spaine, a Margarite, French, *Vn Curtain*; in England, among the barbarous, a Whore; but among the Gentle, their vsuall associates, a Puncke: but now the word refined being latest, and the authority brought from a Climate as yet vnconquered, the fruitfull County of Kent, they call them *Croshabell,* which is a word but lately vsed, and fitting with their trade, being of a louely and courteous condition. Leauing them: This Fantasticke, whose braine was made of nought but Corke and Spunge, came to the cold lodging of Monsieur *Peele*, in his blacke Sattin Sute, his Gowne furred with Coney, in his Slippers: being in the euening, he thought to heare *Georges* booke, and so to returne to his Inne; (this not of the wisest, being of S. *Bernards.*) *George* bids him welcome, told him he would gladly haue his opinion in his booke. He willingly condescended, and *George* begins to read, and betweene euery Sceane he would make pauses, and demand his opinion how he liked the cariage of it. Quoth he, wondrous well, the conueyance. O, but (quoth *George*) the end is farre better: for he meant another conueyance ere they two departed.) *George* was very tedious in reading, and the night grew old: I protest, quoth the Gentleman, I haue stayed ouer-long, I feare me I shall hardly get into mine Inne. If you feare that, quoth *George,* we will haue a cleane paire of sheets, and you take a simple lodging here. This house-gull willingly embraced it, and to bed they goe, where *George* in the midst of the night spying his time, put on this

Dormouse

Dormouse his cloaths, desired God to keepe him in good rest, honestly takes leaue of him and the house, to whom he was indebted foure Nobles. When this Drone awaked, and found himselfe so left, he had not the wit to be angry, but swore scuruily at his misfortune, and said, I thought he would not haue vsed me so. And although it so pleased the Fates he had another sute to put on, yet he could not get thence, till he had paid the mony *George* ought to the house, which for his credit he did: and when he came to his lodging, in anger he made a Poem of it:

> Peele *is no Poet, but a Gull and Clowne,*
> *To take away my Cloaths and Gowne:*
> *I vow by* Ioue, *if I can see him weare it,*
> *Ile giue him a glyg, and patiently beare it.*

How *George Peele* serued halfe a score Citizens.

GEorge once had inuited halfe a score of his friends to a great Supper, where they were passing merry, no cheare wanting, wine enough, musicke playing: the night growing on, and being vpon departure, they call for a reckoning. *George* swears there is not a penny for them to pay. They, being men of good fashion, by no meanes will yeeld vnto it, but euery man throwes downe his money, some ten shillings, some fiue, some more: protesting something they will pay. Well, quoth *George*, taking vp all the mony; seeing you will be so wilfull, you shall see what shall follow: he commands the musicke to play, and while they were skipping and dancing, *George* gets his cloake, sends vp two pottles of Hypocrasse, and leaues them and the reckoning to pay. They wondring at the stay of *George*, meant to be gone, but they were

staid

ſtaid by the way, and before they went, forced to pay the reckoning anew. This ſhewed a minde in him, he cared not whom he deceiued, ſo he profited himſelfe for the preſent.

A Ieſt of *George* going to *Oxford*.

THere was ſome halfe doozen of Citizens, that had oftentimes been ſolliciters with *George*, he being a Maſter of Art at the Uniuerſity of *Oxford*, that he would ride with them to the Commencement, it being at Midſomer. *George*, willing to pleaſure the Gentlemen his friends, rode along with them. When they had rode the better part of the way, they baited at a Village called *Stoken*, fiue miles from *Wickham*: good cheare was beſpoken for dinner, and frolicke was the company, all but *George*, who could not be in that pleaſant veine that did ordinarily poſſeſſe him, by reaſon he was without mony: but he had not fetcht forty turns about the chamber, before his noddle had entertained a conceit how to mony himſelfe with credit, and yet gleane it from ſome one of the company. There was among them one excellent Aſſe, a fellow that did nothing but friſke vp and downe the Chamber, that his mony might be heard chide in his pocket: this fellow had *George* obſerued, and ſecretly conuaied his gilt Rapier and Dagger into another Chamber, and there cloſely hid it: that done, he called vp the Tapſter, and upon his cloake borrowes fiue ſhilling for an houre or ſo, till his man came, (as he could faſhion it well enough:) ſo much mony he had, and then who more merry than *George*? Meat was brought vp, they ſet themſelues to dinner, all full of mirth, eſpecially my little foole, who dranke not of the concluſion of their feaſt: dinner ended, much prattle

paſt

paſt, euery man begins to buckle to his furniture: among whom this Hichcocke miſſed his Rapier: at which all the company were in a maze; he beſides his wits, for he had borrowed it of a ſpeciall friend of his, and ſwore he had rather ſpend 20 Nobles. This is ſtrange, quoth *George*, it ſhould be gone in this faſhion, none being here but our ſelues, and the fellows of the houſe, who were examined, but no Rapier could be heard of: all the company much grieued; but *George* in a pittiful chafe, ſwore it ſhould coſt him forty ſhillings, but he would know what was become of it, if Art could doe it: and with that he cauſed the Oaſtler to ſaddle his Nag, for *George* would ride to a Scholler, a friend of his, that had ſkill in ſuch matters. O, good M. *Peele*, quoth the fellow, want no mony, here is forty ſhillings, ſee what you can doe, and if you pleaſe, Ile ride along with you. Not ſo, quoth *George*, taking his forty ſhillings, Ile ride alone, and be you as merry as you can till my returne. So *George* left them, and rode directly to *Oxford*, there he acquaints a friend of his with all the circumſtance, who preſently tooke Horſe and rode along with him to laugh at the ieſt. When they came backe, *George* tels them he had brought one of the rareſt men in *England*: whom they with much complement bid welcome. He, after a diſtracted countenance, and ſtrange words, takes this Bulfinch by the wriſt, and carried him into the priuy, and there willed him to put in his head, but while he had written his name, and told forty: which he willingly did: that done the Scholar aſked him what he ſaw? By my faith Sir, I ſmelt a villanous ſent, but I ſaw nothing. Then I haue, quoth he, and with that directed him where his Rapier was: ſaying, it is iuſt North-Eaſt, incloſed in wood neare the earth: for which they all made diligent ſearch, till *George*, who hid it under a ſettle, found it; to the comfort of the fellow, the ioy of the company, and the eternall credit, of his friend, who was entertained with wine and sugar; and *George* redeemed his cloake, rode merrily to *Oxford*, hauing coine in his pocket, where this Loach spares not for any expence, for the good fortune he had in the happy finding of his Rapier.

How *George* serued his Hostis.

GEorge lying at an old Widdows house, and had gone so farre on the score, that his credit would stretch no farther; for she had made a vow not to depart with drinke or victuals without ready mony: Which *George* seeing the fury of his froward Hostis, in griefe kept his chamber, called to his Hostis, and told her, she should vnderstand that he was not without mony, how poorely soeuer he appeared to her, and that my diet shall testifie: in the meane time, good Hostis, quoth he, send for such a friend of mine. She did, so his friend came, to whom *George* imparted his minde, the effect whereof was this, to pawne his Cloake, Hose and Doublet, vnknowne to his Hostis: for, quoth *George*, this seuen nights doe I intend to keepe my bed. (Truly he spake, for his intent was, the bed should not keepe him any longer.) Away goes he to pawne his apparell; *George* bespeakes good cheere to supper; which was no shamble-butchers stuffe, but according to the place: for, his Chamber being remote from the house, at the end of the Garden, his apparell being gone, it appeared to him as the Counter, therefore to comfort himselfe, he dealt in Poultry. His friend brought the mony, supped with him, his Hostis he very liberally paid, but cauilled with her at her vnkindnesse; vowing that while he lay there, none should attend him but his friend. The Hostis replied, a Gods name, she was well contented with

it:

it: so was *George* too: for none knew better than himselfe what he intended, but in briefe, thus he vsed his kind Hostis. After his apparrell and mony was gone, he made bold with the Feather-bed he lay on, which his friend slily conueyed away, hauing as villanous a Wolfe in his belly as *George*, though not altogether so wise, for that Feather-bed they deuoured in two dayes, feathers and all: which was no sooner digested, but away went the Couerlet, Sheets, and the Blanket; and at the last dinner, when *Georges* good friend perceiuing nothing left but the bed-cords, as the Deuill would haue it, straight came in his mind the fashion of a halter, the foolish kind knaue would needs fetch a quart of sacke for his friend *George*; which sacke to this day neuer saw Vintners Cellar: and so he left *George* in a cold Chamber, a thin shirt, a rauished bed, no comfort left him, but the bare bones of deceased Capons. In this distresse *George* bethought him what he might doe, nothing was left him; and his eye wandered vp and downe the empty Chamber, by chance he spied out an old Armor, at which sight *George* was the ioyfullest man in Christendome, for the Armour of *Achilles*, that *Vlysses* and *Aiax* stroue for, was not more precious to them, than this to him: for he presently claps it vpon his backe, the Halbert in his hand, the Moryon on his head, and so gets out the backe way, marches from Shorditch to Clarkenwell, to the no small wonder of those spectators that beheld him. Being arriued to the wished hauen he would be, an old acquaintance of his furnished him with an old Sute, and an old Cloake for his old Armour. How the Hostis looked when she saw that metamorphosis in her chamber, iudge those Bomborts that liue by tapping, between the age of fifty and threescore.

D 2 How

How he serued a Tapster.

GEorge was making merry with three or foure of his friends in Pye-corner, where the Tapster of the house was much giuen to Poetry: for he had ingroſſed the Knight of the Sunne, *Venus* and *Adonis*, and other Pamphlets which the ſtrippling had collected together, and knowing George to be a Poet, he tooke great delight in his company, and out of his bounty would beſtow a brace of Cannes of him. *George* obſeruing the humour of the Tapſter, meant preſently to worke vpon him. What will you ſay, quoth *George* to his friends, if out of this ſpirit of the Cellar I fetch a good Angell that ſhall bid vs all to ſupper. Wee would gladly ſee that, quoth his friends. Content your ſelfe, quoth *George*. The Tapſter aſcends with his two Cannes, deliuers one to M. *Peele*, and the other to his friends, giues them kinde welcome: but *George* in ſtead of giuing him thanks, bids him not to trouble him, and begins in theſe termes. I proteſt, Gentlemen, I wonder you will vrge me ſo much, I ſweare I haue it not about me. What is the matter, quoth the Tapſter, hath any one angered you? No faith, quoth *George*, Ile tell thee, it is this: There is a friend of ours in Newgate, for nothing but onely the command of the Juſtices, and he being now to be releaſed, ſends to me to bring him an Angell: Now the man I loue dearely well, and if he want ten Angels, he ſhall haue them, for I know him ſure: but heres the miſery, either I muſt goe home, or I muſt be forced to pawne this, and plucks an old Harry groat out of his pocket. The Tapſter lookes vpon it: Why, and it pleaſe you Sir, quoth he, this is but a groat. No Sir, quoth *George*, I know it is but a groat: but this groat will I not loſe for forty pounds: for this groat had I of my Mother,

as

as a testimony of a Lease of a house I am to possesse after her decease: and if I should lose this groat, I were in a faire case: and either I must pawne this groat, or there the fellow must lie still. Quoth the Tapster, If it please you, I will lend you an Angell on it, and I will assure you it shall be safe. Wilt thou, quoth *George*? as thou art an honest man, locke it vp in thy Chest, and let me haue it whensoeuer I call for it. As I am an honest man, you shall, quoth the Tapster. *George* deliuered him his groat: the Tapster gaue him ten shillings: to the Tauerne goe they with the mony, and there merrily spend it. It fell out in a small time after, the Tapster, hauing many of these lurches, fell to decay, and indeed was turned out of seruice, hauing no more coine in the world than this groat; and in this misery he met *George* as poore as himselfe. O sir, quoth the Tapster, you are happily met; I haue your groat safe, though since I saw you last, I haue bid great extremity; and I protest, saue that groat, I haue not one penny in the world; Therefore I pray you Sir, helpe me to my mony, and take your pawne. Not for the world, quoth *George*; thou saist thou hast but that groat in the world, my bargaine was, that thou shouldst keepe that groat vntill I did demand it of thee: I aske thee none. I will do thee more good, because thou art an honest fellow, keepe thou that groat still, till I call for it: and so doing, the proudest Jacke in *England* cannot iustifie thou art not worth a groat, otherwise they might: and so, honest *Michael*, farewell. So *George* leaues the poor Tapster picking of his fingers, his head full of proclamations what he might doe: at last sighing he ends with this Prouerbe:

For the price of a barrel of Beere,
I haue bought a groats-worth of wit,
Is not that deare?

How

How *George* serued a Gentlewoman.

GEorge vsed often to an Ordnary in this Towne, where a kinswoman of the good wifes in the house, held a great pride and vaine opinion of her own mother-wit: for her tongue was as a Jack continually wagging: and for she had heard that *George* was a Scholler, she thought she would find a time to giue him notice, that she had as much in her head, as euer was in her Grandfathers: yet in some things she differed from the women of those dayes: for their naturall complexion was their beauty: now this Titmouse, what she is scanted by nature, she doth replenish by Art, as her boxes of red and white daily can testifie. But to come to *George*, who arriued at the Ordnary among other Gallants, throwes his cloake vpon the Table, salutes the Gentlemen, and presently calls for a cup of Canary. *George* had a paire of Hose on, that for some offence durst not bee seene in that hue they were first dyed in, but from his first colour being a youthfull green, his long age turned him into a mournfull black, and for his antiquity was in print: which this busie body perceiuing, thought now to giue it him to the quicke: and drawing neere M. *Peele*, looking vpon his breeches, By my troth, Sir, quoth shee, these are exceedingly well printed. At which word, *George* being a little moued in his mind, that his old Hose were called in question, answered, and by my faith, Mistris, quoth *George*, your face is most damnably ill painted. How mean you Sir, quoth shee? Marry thus, Mistris, quoth *George*, That if it were not for printing and painting, my arse and your face would grow out of reparations. At which shee biting her lip, in a parat fury went downe the staires. The Gentlemen laughed at the sudden answer of *George*, and being seated at dinner, the Gentlemen would needes haue the company of this witty Gentlewoman to dine with them; who with little denying came, in hope to cry quittance with *George*. When shee was ascended, the Gentlemen would needes place her by M. *Peele*; because they did vse to dart one at another, they thought it meet, for their more safety, they should bee placed neerest together. *George* kindly entertains her: and being seated, he desires her to reach him the Capon that stood by her, and he would be so bold as to carue for his mony: and as she put out her arme to take the Capon, *George* sitting by her, yerks me out a huge fart, which made all the company in a maze, one looking vpon the other, yet they knew it came that way. Peace, quoth *George*, and iogs her on the elbow, I will say it was I. At which all the Company fell into a huge laughter, shee into a fretting fury, vowing neuer she should sleepe quietly till she was reuenged of *George* his wrong done vnto her: and so in a great chafe left their company.

FINIS.

J. Smeeton, Printer, 148, St. Martin's Lane.

THE BORROWER WILL BE CHARGED
AN OVERDUE FEE IF THIS BOOK IS
NOT RETURNED TO THE LIBRARY ON
OR BEFORE THE LAST DATE STAMPED
BELOW. NON-RECEIPT OF OVERDUE
NOTICES DOES NOT EXEMPT THE
BORROWER FROM OVERDUE FEES.

Harvard College Widener Library
Cambridge, MA 02138 (617) 495-2413

SEP 1 0 2001

STALL-STUDY
CHARGE

Check Out More Titles From HardPress Classics Series In this collection we are offering thousands of classic and hard to find books. This series spans a vast array of subjects – so you are bound to find something of interest to enjoy reading and learning about.

Subjects:
Architecture
Art
Biography & Autobiography
Body, Mind &Spirit
Children & Young Adult
Dramas
Education
Fiction
History
Language Arts & Disciplines
Law
Literary Collections
Music
Poetry
Psychology
Science
…and many more.

Visit us at www.hardpress.net

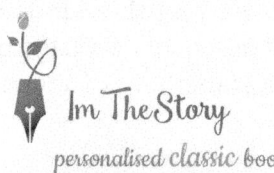

Im TheStory
personalised classic books

"Beautiful gift.. lovely finish.
My Niece loves it, so precious!"

Helen R Brumfieldon

★★★★★

FOR KIDS, PARTNERS
AND FRIENDS

Timeless books such as:

Alice in Wonderland • The Jungle Book • The Wonderful Wizard of Oz
Peter and Wendy • Robin Hood • The Prince and The Pauper
The Railway Children • Treasure Island • A Christmas Carol

Romeo and Juliet • Dracula

Visit
Im TheStory.com
and order yours today!

WS - #0023 - 050324 - C0 - 229/152/3 - PB - 9780371553664 - Gloss Lamination